Whānau

Reo Māori phrases to share
with the people you love

WRITTEN BY DONOVAN TE AHUNUI FARNHAM
ILLUSTRATED BY REHUA WILSON

MOA
PRESS

To my beloved wife, whose strength and determination have pushed us to make te reo Māori a living, breathing part of our home.

—Donovan

To whānau in all its forms – those we are born to, those we choose and those who choose us. May these expressions be a bridge of connection and love, brought to life through the beauty of te reo Māori.

—Rehua

A Moa Press Book
Published in Aotearoa New Zealand and Australia in 2025 by Moa Press
(an imprint of Hachette Aotearoa New Zealand Limited)
Level 2, 23 O'Connell Street, Auckland, New Zealand
www.moapress.co.nz
www.hachette.co.nz

A catalogue record for this book is available from the National Library of New Zealand.

978-1-86971-499-4 (hardback)

Cover and internal design by Maimoa Creative
Printed in China by 1010 Printing International Limited

He Rārangi Wāhanga

Contents

Introduction

I have worked with children for over twenty years and now more than ever I'm being asked, where do I start with learning te reo Māori? The best place to start is wherever your whānau is. That might be at home next to the people you feel most comfortable with, or with a community of people who are also at the beginning of their Māori-language learning journey – regardless, learning and sharing with your whānau will help strengthen your own learning, while making it more meaningful.

Whānau is often translated as "extended family" or "kinship group". It encapsulates the wider sense of family that includes all the different branches of your whakapapa, your genealogy, as well as those that you have a close relationship with, even if they are not related by blood.

In short, whānau is about those closest to you, and this book has been created in the hope that you will share it with those you love most.

Nāku, nā
Te Ahunui

1

He Kōrero Aroha mā te Whānau

Words of Aroha for your Whānau

There is no single word in English that completely encompasses the concept of aroha in te ao Māori. It can be the love you feel for your partner, friends and family, and it is also kindness and compassion, empathy and sympathy. Aroha becomes clear when we start looking deeper into the language that is used to interact with our whānau. This first chapter offers a collection of heartfelt messages to share with your loved ones.

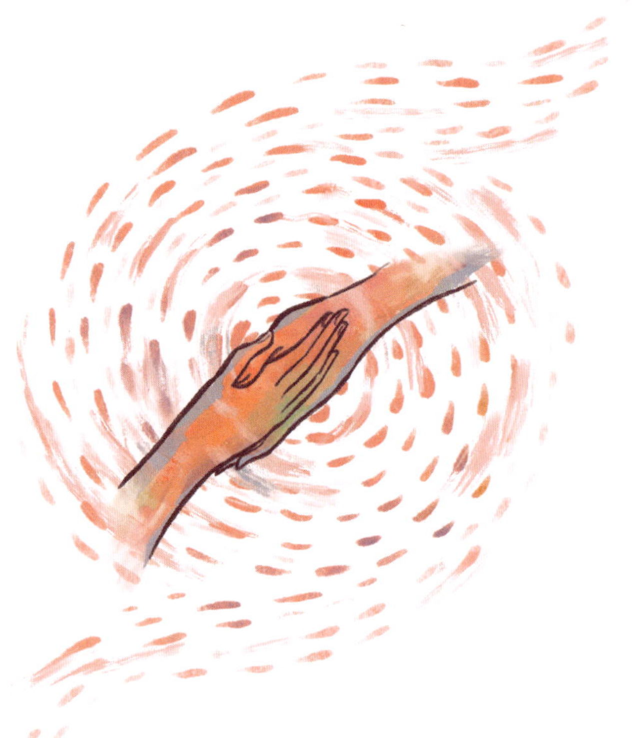

E te tau

Sweetheart

This term can be shared between partners and is often prefaced with a greeting, like "Kia ora, e te tau". Another way to use it is from a parent speaking to their child.

E te tōrere

True love

This is an endearment for your one and only true love or romantic partner. It acknowledges your lasting affection and passionate, fulfilling relationship.

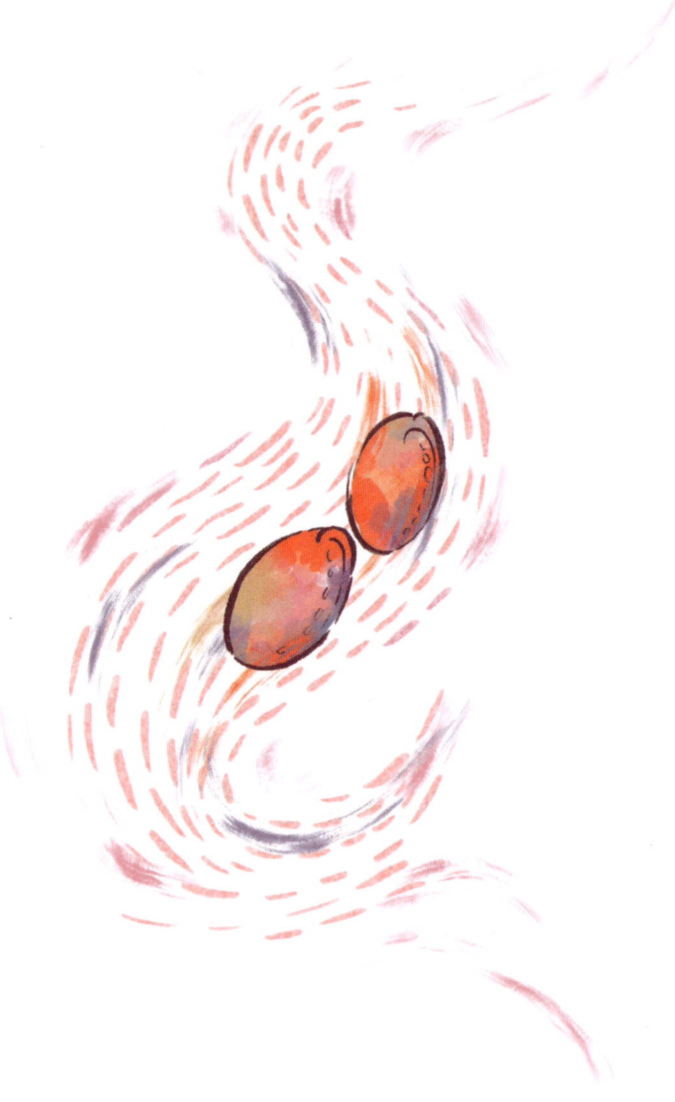

E te piri pāua

Partner in crime

The **pāua** is known for how well it clings to underwater rocks. Here, the term is used to describe two people who are inseparable.

E te rātā whakamaru

Protector

Rātā whakamaru likens a protector in the whānau to how the rātā, a large tree with crimson flowers and hard red timber, offers protection to all the plants and creatures in the forest below.

E te kāhu kōrako

Wise one

The **kāhu kōrako** (the white-feathered hawk) is a metaphor for our elders. This metaphor stems from a proverb which advises to travel under the guidance of a knowledgeable elder, **"me haere i raro i te kāhu kōrako, kia kai i te kai, kia whiwhi i te taonga"**.

E te rearea

My high achiever

This expression comes from a proverb, "he iti rearea teitei kahikatea ka taea" (even the small bellbird can ascend to the great heights of the kahikatea tree). Here, you're comparing someone, such as a child in your whānau, to the rearea that can achieve lofty goals.

E te ringa raupā

Hard worker

The term **ringa raupā** comes from a proverb that describes marrying someone with calloused hands, “**moea te ringa raupā**”. Traditionally, a person with callouses on their hands is considered a hard worker.

E te kuru pounamu

My precious jewel

Kuru pounamu refers to a small piece of treasured greenstone, but it can also describe a child who is deeply loved and cherished by their family.

E aku awhi rito

My parents

The way the leaves of the **harakeke**, the flax plant, grow represents a whānau. In the centre is the **rito** (smaller shoot), while on either side of this shoot are the **awhi rito** (the parents), and the outer leaves represent the **tūpuna** (the grandparents and ancestors).

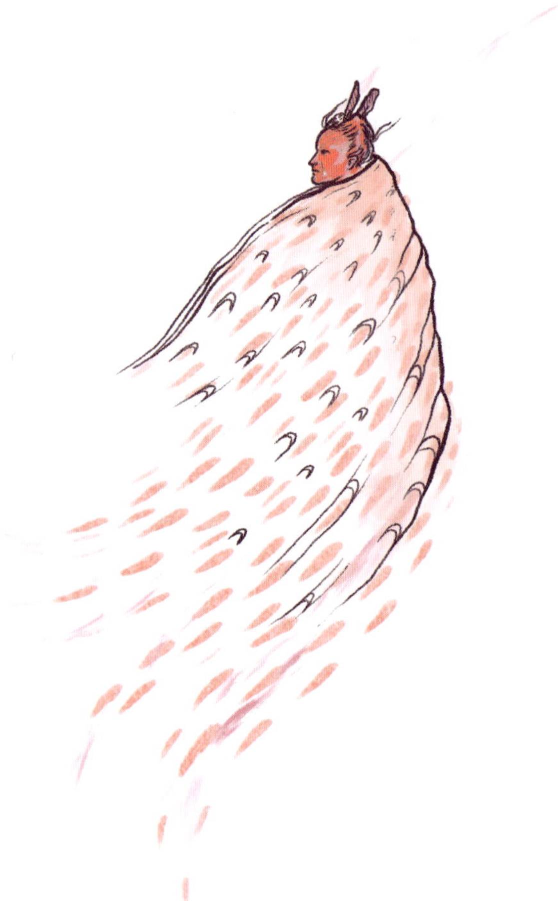

E te iho pūmanawa

My role model

Iho pūmanawa refers to a person who is naturally talented and clever. In modern usage, an iho pūmanawa is someone that is looked up to and admired.

He manawa tītī

A relentless person

This expression likens someone to the tītī (muttonbird), which is well known in te ao Māori for its determination – it covers great distances during its migration and puts up a long fight when hunted.

He toka tū moana

A stalwart

A **toka tū moana** is a rock that can be seen protruding from the ocean. Despite rough seas, the rock remains steadfastly in the same place. **"He toka tū moana"** is a lovely way of describing someone who is reliable.

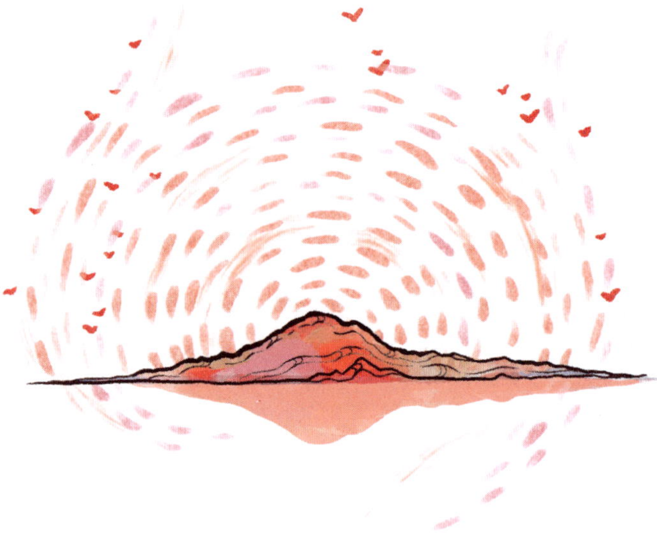

He whakaaio whenua

A peacemaker

Whakaaio refers to bringing peace, and **whakaaio whenua** can be interpreted as calming the lands. This is a genuine phrase to use for someone who can bring harmony in turbulent situations and maintain that peace.

He kanohi hōmiromiro

Someone with an eye for detail

Like the **hōmiromiro** (tomtit), which is known for its keen eyesight, this term describes someone who is scrupulous, or a person who has a knack for seeing the small details.

He kiri tuna

A person who is thick-skinned

This term likens a person to the thick-skinned tuna to imply that they aren't sensitive to criticism or insults.

He waewae kai kapua

A traveller or adventurer

This expression comes from a proverb that refers to a risk-taker being able to succeed over a more accomplished, yet cautious, person. In full, the proverb is "kāore e tae te waewae kai pakiaka ki te waewae kai kapua".

He korokoro tūī

A beautiful singer

The **tūī** is known for its ability to mimic the alluring calls of the other birds, and this expression compares the dulcet tones of a beautiful singer to the tūī's song.

He arero taiaha

A diplomatic speaker

An **arero taiaha** refers to someone who has the tongue of a **taiaha**. The taiaha is a staff-like traditional Māori weapon, usually with a carved head on the end and a protruding tongue. The carved head is often double-sided and is used as an example of someone who can see matters from both sides while remaining impartial.

He kaiurungi

A leader

The **kaiurungi** is the steerer of the **waka**, and the term can be used for someone who is a navigator or leads others.

He ihupuku

A novice

Ihupuku has many different interpretations. It can refer to inexperience or to someone who is eager to learn. In your whānau, mentoring can take many shapes, but it's all about navigating new adventures and learning experiences.

2

Te Whakapuaki Kare ā-Roto

Talking About Feelings

Our Māori ancestors were very in touch with their **kare ā-roto**, their emotions. For both men and women, it was common for tears to be shed and wails to be heard, both in the spirit of joy and sadness, when seeing one another after long periods of time. Matters of the heart were also freely shared and not hidden away. It's important to be unreserved in expressing our feelings for our whānau and those close to us.

Ka nui taku ora

I'm very well

When asked "**kei te pēhea koe?**" (how are you?) most people usually answer with "**kei te pai ahau**" (I am good), but if you'd like to add a little more enthusiasm, you could say "**ka nui taku ora**" (I'm very well).

Kua pau te hau

Completely exhausted

"Kua pau te hau" is a common saying in te reo Māori when someone is feeling overworked and exhausted. This lets people know that your energy is low.

E ngākau whakapuke ana au

I am feeling enthusiastic

Ngākau refers to your heart or the seat of your affections, while **whakapuke** speaks to the rising of your feelings; therefore, the term **ngākau whakapuke** can be interpreted as having a heart brimming with emotions.

E koa ana te ngākau

I'm elated

Here, you're letting people know that your heart is happy or that you're ecstatic.

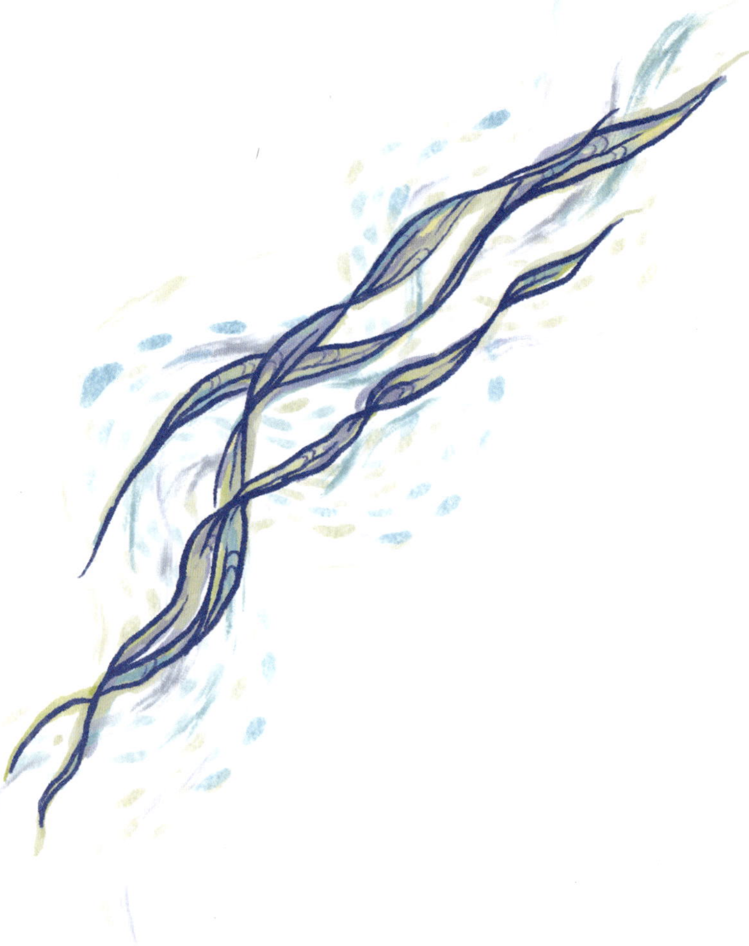

E rimu pae noa ana

Feeling unsettled (or at a loss)

Rimu pae noa is seaweed that drifts through the ocean, and it can be used to describe someone who is a bit of a wanderer or the feeling of being at a loss.

E tohetaka ana au

I'm feeling lazy

The **tohetaka** (native dandelion) doesn't open up until the day is half over, so it is used to describe people who are lazy or sleepyheads.

E warea ana e te moe

Falling asleep

This term refers to being so sleepy that you can no longer stay awake. If you want to ask someone if they're falling asleep, you might pose the question, "E warea ana koe e te moe?"

E rau kahakaha ana au

I'm feeling anxious (or excited)

Rau kahakaha are the leaves of the perching lily, which flap and dance about when the wind blows, so this expression likens feeling agitated, excited or anxious to these dancing leaves.

Me he pārera maunu au

I'm out of my depth

This expression comes from the saying "**he pārera maunu ki te kau i te moana**" (a moulting duck swimming in the ocean). The **pārera** (grey duck) is known for swimming in shallow waters and is out of its depth in the ocean.

E tōtara wāhi rua ana

I'm undecided

This expression comes from a proverb, "he tōtara wāhi rua he kai nā te ahi" (split wood is food for the fire). This proverb is used to caution groups who need to show solidarity, or people who are undecided, by referencing the way split wood burns more quickly. In modern usage, "tōtara wāhi rua" is said by a person who is sitting on the fence or in two minds about a decision.

Mō taku hē

I'm sorry for my error

This is a general apology for having done something wrong, but other phrases can be used for specific situations. If you've arrived late, you can say "mō taku tōmuri". If you're worried about bothering someone, use "mō taku whakapōrearea", and if you'd like to apologise for something you might have done to someone else, try saying "aku whakapāha".

Taku hē, taku hē

My mistake

Often in te reo Māori, words, phrases, or even parts of words are repeated to show emphasis. You'll notice that **taku hē** is used twice; this is said as a gentle admission of your error.

Ka aroha kē hoki

That's so sad

Ka aroha kē hoki can be used to convey sympathy or empathy. You could say this to someone who is disappointed to show that you understand and empathise with them.

I wāu nei hoki

You poor thing

Whether you're helping someone who has fallen over, or dealing with someone who feels hard done by, this can be said in either an earnest or a sarcastic manner.

Kei māharahara

Don't worry

Using **kei** before an action can signal that it shouldn't be done. Other phrases in this form include **kei taka** (don't fall), **kei tangi** (don't cry) and **kei āmaimai** (don't be nervous).

Tē taea te pēhea

It can't be helped

This phrase is for those moments when you can only throw your hands up and say, "nothing can be done about it!" Sometimes, no matter how much effort you put into something, all you can say is, "tē taea te pēhea".

E mārama ana

So be it

E mārama ana lets someone know that you understand that it is what it is.

Kua puta te ihu

It's been accomplished

Kua puta te ihu is a phrase traditionally used to talk about escaping from danger. In modern te reo Māori, this is a common saying to talk about completing a heavy workload or even graduating.

Kia manawanui mai

Thank you for your patience

My reo Māori teacher, Pānia Papa, calls the kia at the beginning of this type of phrase "the wishing particle". We see it in examples such as kia ora, which is a greeting, but can also be used to wish someone well. Say "kia manawanui mai" when you're asking someone to be patient with you.

Kei taku āhuru mōwai ahau

I'm in my happy place

There's nothing quite like your happy place, the one space in which you feel at home, your safe haven. This is your āhuru mōwai.

3

Hei Whakatītina i te Whānau

Encouraging the Whānau

The concept of **mihi** (acknowledgements) is widely seen in te ao Māori to recognise and encourage one another. In both formal settings, such as **whaikōrero** (formal speech making), and informal settings, it's not uncommon to see people stand up and show their appreciation for each other.

Rehe ake nei

You're so talented

A ringa rehe is an acknowledgement of someone who is skilled at working with their hands, and the structure ake nei is used to express the epitome of something. So, when we use the phrase rehe ake nei, we're literally saying that you couldn't be more skilful.

Kātahi te tamaiti mākohakoha ko koe

You're such a generous child

This is another example where you can substitute mākohakoha for another describing word to praise a child. If you said "kātahi te tamaiti hūmārie ko koe", you'd be acknowledging how humble your tamaiti is.

Ka wani kē koe

You're a genius

This idiom can be used on its own to talk about how clever someone is, or you can use it to comment on something. If you said "ka wani kē tō mahi", you'd be complimenting a person's work. You can also replace mahi with any other noun to applaud someone's efforts.

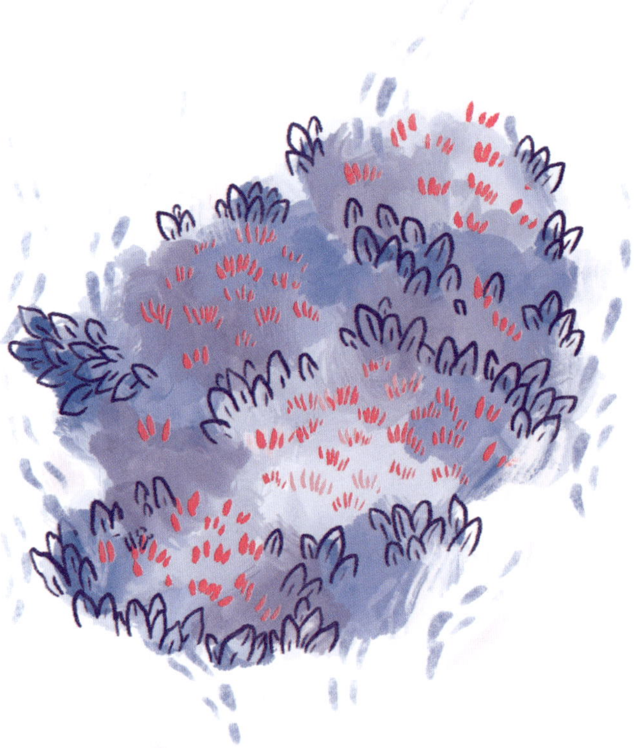

Kei whea mai

That's outstanding

This expression is used to say how amazing something is. If you'd like to comment on how outstanding someone is, you could say "kei whea atu i a koe" directly to them.

Inā te ātaahua

How beautiful

Inā te is a versatile starter used to emphasise the quality of something. By adding different descriptions at the end, you can change what you're acknowledging. Here, the word **ātaahua** can be substituted with other words, for example, **inā te reka!** (how delicious!) or **inā te kounga!** (what quality!).

Tō atamai hoki

You're so clever

The structure of **tō atamai hoki** can be used with a number of describing words. Here, **atamai**, meaning clever, could be substituted with other Māori words. You could say "**tō tapatapahi hoki**" to tell someone how stylish they are, or "**tō pukumahi hoki**" to comment on how hard they've been working.

Rarawe noa iho

That looked effortless

This saying has many English language interpretations, such as easy-peasy, or, it'll be a walk in the park. Rarawe noa iho can also be used in response to a request, letting someone know that you can easily do what they're asking.

He waha kākākura

A great speaker

Kākā are known for their cry, and the leader of a flock, the **kākākura**, is the most impressive of all. When someone in your whānau speaks for you, you can use this expression to mean they have the voice of a leader, like the kākākura.

Mei kore ake koe

Thank goodness you're here

This is a saying that acknowledges the importance of someone's contribution, to the point where a task might not be achievable without them.

Hūkere, hūkere

Get stuck in

Hūkere means to paddle vigorously. It refers to the encouragement used on the waka to urge fellow paddlers to put extra effort into their work.

AROHA
MAI

Kikino kē rā koe

You're onto it

Kikino usually means bad or evil; however, in this saying, it's used to praise someone who has hit the nail on the head.

E tū i te tū a te uru kahikatea

Let's stick together

This expression instructs us to stand as a grove of **kahikatea** trees. The kahikatea are our tallest native trees, which are always found in groves together – they never stand alone.

Karawhiua

Go for it

While saying **karawhiua** on its own is an encouragement for someone to give it their all, it's often seen in the expression "**karawhiua mō te hemo tonu atu**", which can be interpreted as "give it everything you've got".

Ka rawe te mahi tahi

Great teamwork

Mahi tahi is an important concept in the Māori world. It means to work as one. Mahi tahi is an important concept in te ao Māori, and is deeply valued as critical to success in traditional Māori society.

Me pūrua te moko

Let's go over that again

In the Māori art of **tā moko**, **pūrua i te moko** means to redraw over the moko again.

Me poho kererū

Be proud

This phrase recalls the kererū and how it always looks proud when it's standing on a branch with its chest puffed up and prominent.

Me tohe puruhi

Be persistent

In using this expression, you'll encourage someone to be like a flea, which is recognised for its persistence and tenacity.

Kia kūmara tonu

Stay humble

There is a Māori proverb that states "kāore te kūmara e kōrero mō tōna ake reka" – "the kūmara doesn't speak of its own sweetness". Kia kūmara means be like a kūmara; that is, don't speak about your own success.

Tūwhitia te hopo

Feel the fear and do it anyway

Reo Māori champion Te Wharehuia Milroy once said, "Tūwhitia te hopo, mairangatia te angitu" or, "Overcome your fears to achieve". Today the shortened version, tūwhitia te hopo, is used by many throughout Aotearoa as an encouragement to push through self-doubt.

Kei mate wheke

Never surrender

This idiom comes from a longer proverb, "kaua e mate wheke, me mate ururoa" or, "don't die like the octopus, die like the shark". Octopuses have a reputation for not putting up a fight when they're caught, whereas sharks don't give up, no matter what!

4

Te Whakanui me te Tautoko i tō Whānau

Celebrating and Supporting your Whānau

Whanaungatanga signifies your deep connection to your whānau, as well as the close relationships you foster with others through collaboration and shared experiences. Empathising with those in your community builds whanaungatanga – as these bonds are strengthened and cultivated, you grow in harmony with each other and become interconnected and interdependent. Whanaungatanga is the foundation upon which safety and belonging are built, and though it was a matter of survival in traditional Māori communities, reinforcing whanaungatanga today helps us to achieve more.

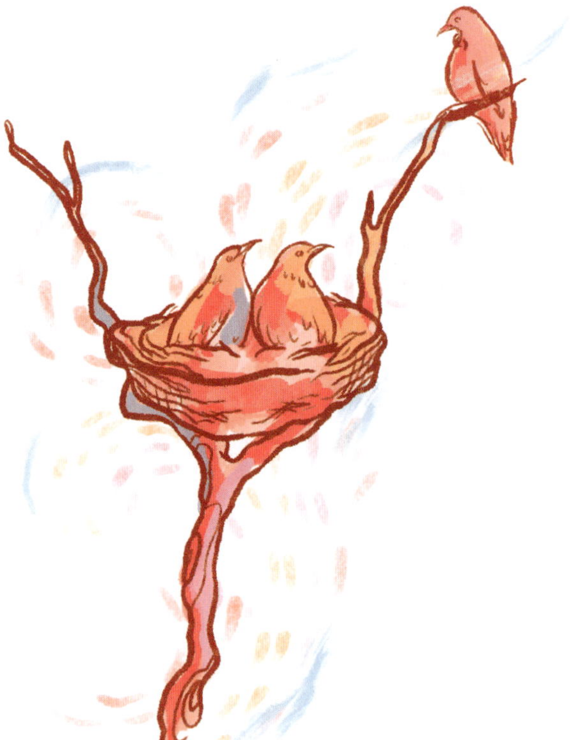

Nau mai

Welcome

If you'd like to be more specific, you can let people know where or what they're being welcomed to using ki. You could say "nau mai ki taku whare" if you'd like to welcome someone to your house, or "nau mai ki te whānau" if you'd like to welcome them to the family.

He koanga ngākau, he rūnga manawa te kite i a koe

So happy to see you

He koanga ngākau, he rūnga manawa te kite i a koe lets someone know that your heart is jumping for joy to see them.

Ka nui te mihi i tō manaaki mai

Thank you for your hospitality

The principle of manaakitanga (hospitality and the duty of care) is of the utmost importance in te ao Māori. As a guest, you can show manaakitanga by bringing koha (gifts) and respecting the customs of the hosts. Here, you can thank someone who has been looking after you.

Hari huritau

Happy birthday

Birthdays are a wonderful excuse to bring the whānau together. Wish someone a happy birthday by saying **hari huritau**. If you'd like to sing happy birthday to someone in te reo Māori, here are the lyrics:

Hari huritau ki a koe, Hari huritau ki a koe,
Hari huritau ki a ________, Hari huritau ki a koe.

E mihi ana

E mihi ana

Thanks/Congratulations

E mihi ana is very broad and can be used in many contexts, from saying thank you to congratulating someone on a recent success.

E rikarika ana te
ngākau ki te kite i a koe

E rikarika ana te ngākau ki te kite i a koe

Can't wait to see you

Rikarika is another term to show excitement. Show someone how excited you are to see them by messaging them and letting them know.

Kua mahana te whare i a koutou katoa

Thank you all for coming

Here, you're letting a group of people you're hosting know that your house has been warmed due to their presence, as a way of thanking them for coming.

He iti nā te aroha

Something small as a gesture of aroha

This phrase is commonly used with giving a koha, a gift. A koha is a symbol of aroha, whether it be contributing kai to the meal, helping out a friend in need or contributing money to the marae.

Kua hinga te tōtara

A mighty tōtara has fallen

In traditional Māori laments, the expression "**kua hinga te tōtara i te wao nui a Tāne**" (a mighty tōtara has fallen in Tāne's great forest) is used when someone great has passed.

Hanga aroha ana

That's heartbreaking

Let people know that you see the depth of their worry and sadness. If you'd like to show sympathy upon hearing some news, you could say "hanga aroha ana tēnā rongo".

Ko koe kei te mata o aku mahara

I'm thinking of you

Let someone know that they're at the forefront of your mind by saying "ko koe kei te mata o aku mahara".

Kua ora au i tō peka mai

Your visit is just what I needed

The use of **kua ora** here speaks to a change from not doing so well, to feeling better. Here, you're telling someone that their visit has made you well again.

He kokonga whare ka kitea, he kokonga ngākau e kore e kitea

I'm here for you

This is a Māori proverb that can be interpreted as "while the corners of the house are seen, the corners of the heart aren't seen". It can be used to remind people to take care when engaging with others, as you might not be aware what's really happening for them.

He kitenga kanohi

A familiar face

This phrase has been taken from the Māori proverb "he kitenga kanohi, he hokinga mahara, he koanga ngākau" (seeing a familiar face brings with it happy memories). It is the perfect way to acknowledge a member of your whānau that you haven't seen for a while.

Mānawatia a Matariki

Happy Matariki

Māori follow a lunisolar calendar and celebrate the new year around the middle of winter, though this relies on when certain stars can be seen. Matariki is a time to reflect on the past twelve months, while planning for the year ahead.

Whāia te iti kahurangi

Follow your dreams

This is a shortened version of the Māori proverb "whāia te iti kahurangi, ki te tuohu koe, me he maunga teitei" (aim for the greatest treasure, despite the difficulties). This can be used to encourage someone to pursue their goals.

E pao, tōrea

It's now or never

This expression comes from the proverb "ka whati te tai, ka pao te tōrea" (when the tide recedes, the oystercatcher strikes). The tōrea can be found busily probing for shellfish as the tide is going out, making the most of the opportunity provided to it.

Hei te wā tītoki

See you in due course

The **tītoki** tree bears fruit irregularly. Some years, the tītoki tree fruits plentifully, while in other years, the fruit is scarce. Like the fruit of the tītoki, you might not know when you'll see someone again.

Haere tū atu, hoki tū mai

Safe travels

This is a saying to farewell someone. It lets them know that you hope they will return in good health.

Kāore he painga i a koe

You're the best

This is a shortened version of the expression "mō te ..., kāore he painga i a koe" (when it comes to ..., there's no one better than you). Thank someone for their hospitality by saying "mō te manaaki, kāore he painga i a koe".

E kore e mimiti taku aroha ki a koe

My love for you is endless

"E kore e mimiti taku aroha ki a koe" can be said to anyone you love deeply.

Ngā Mātāpuna

Sources

I consider myself incredibly fortunate to have had the best teachers and mentors in te reo Māori, who continue to inspire me. Added to my insatiable appetite for consuming any reo Māori book I can find, and the wealth of knowledge from the hundreds of newspapers documented by our pioneering Māori authors, these experiences have provided the foundations of this book.

He Mihi

Acknowledgements

There are four pillars who have influenced me in my journey through te ao Māori: Hēmi Dale, who showed me what true passion for te reo Māori looks like; Leon Blake, who embodies cheeky humility; Sir Tīmoti Kāretu, who epitomises the idea of a lifelong learner; and Pānia Papa, who continues to guide me, challenge me and make time for me.

To my amazing editors, Dr Karena Kelly and Dom Visini, and my publisher, Alison Shucksmith: thank you for turning my chaos into clarity and making me look far more polished and professional than I deserve!

Few people know this, but my wife is the one who pushed me to reclaim my heritage language. I have much to thank her for, but making our home and whānau bilingual is at the top of the list.

Donovan Te Ahunui Farnham

Donovan is a reo Māori teacher, a consultant and a strategic leader in Māori-medium education. His education was through the medium of te reo Māori, from kōhanga reo, through to university. Donovan is an alumnus of the University of Auckland (Bachelor of Education: Huarahi Māori Specialisation) and Te Wānanga o Aotearoa (Te Panekiretanga o te Reo). He is also a licensed interpreter and translator of the Māori language (Māori Language Commission).

Rehua Wilson

Rehua specialises in designing immersive spatial experiences with a background in architecture. Her skills in making spaces into visual stories have expanded into the world of print, where she also illustrates books with a specific focus on te ao Māori themes. She was a runner-up for the Margaret Mahy Illustration Prize in 2020.

A Note on the Typeface

Whānau is set in a typeface called Family. Family was released in 2023 by Klim Type Foundry and is based on another font called Clearface, keeping all of Clearface's easy-going curves and idiosyncrasies while updating it for modern use. It's a beautiful, fitting typeface for a book to be shared with whānau – family.